W9-CLQ-648

A FIRST LOOK AT ANIMALS WITH BACKBONES

By Millicent E. Selsam and Joyce Hunt

ILLUSTRATED BY HARRIET SPRINGER

J
596
S

WALKER AND COMPANY ☀ NEW YORK

40709

Library of Congress Cataloging in Publication Data

Selsam, Millicent Ellis, 1912–
   A first look at animals with backbones.

   SUMMARY: An introduction to the characteristics of
the major groups of vertebrates: fish, amphibians,
reptiles, birds, and mammals.
   1. Vertebrates—Juvenile literature.
[1. Vertebrates]   I. Hunt, Joyce, joint author.
II. Springer, Harriet.   III. Title
QL605.3.S44   1978   596   78-4321
ISBN 0-8027-6338-3
ISBN 0-8027-6339-1 lib. bdg.

Text Copyright © 1978 by Millicent E. Selsam and Joyce Hunt
Illustrations Copyright © 1978 by Harriett Springer

All rights reserved. No part of this book may
be reproduced or transmitted in any form or by
any means, electric or mechanical, including
photocopying, recording, or by any information
storage and retrieval system, without permission
in writing from the Publisher.

First published in the United States of America
in 1978 by the Walker Publishing Company, Inc.

Published simultaneously in Canada by Beaverbooks,
Limited, Pickering, Ontario.

Trade ISBN: 0-8027-6338-3
Reinf. ISBN: 0-8027-6339-1
Library of Congress Catalog Card Number: 78-4321

Printed in the United States of America

10 9 8 7 6 5 4 3 2 1

A *FIRST LOOK AT* SERIES

Each of the nature books for this series is planned to develop the child's powers of observation and give him or her a rudimentary grasp of scientific classification.

To the Children in Project Achieve

There are lots of animals in the world.
Some have backbones.
Some do not.

A backbone is a row of bones under the skin
along the middle of the back.
Other bones are attached to it and make up the skeleton.

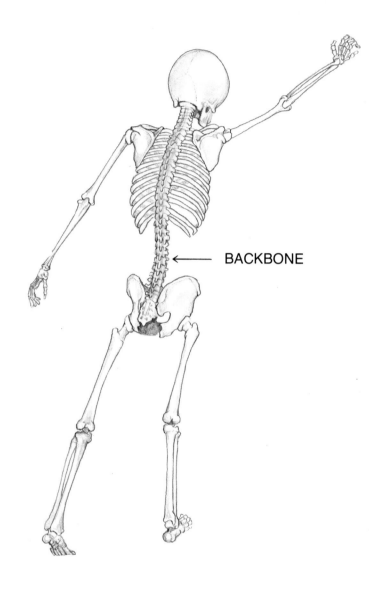

BACKBONE

This is what your skeleton looks like.

You can feel your own backbone.
Bend down and then reach behind you
to feel the bones in the middle of your back.

Any animal that has a backbone is called a vertebrate (VER-ti-brate).

Are you a vertebrate?

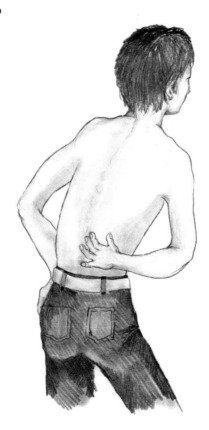

Do any of these animals have a backbone?

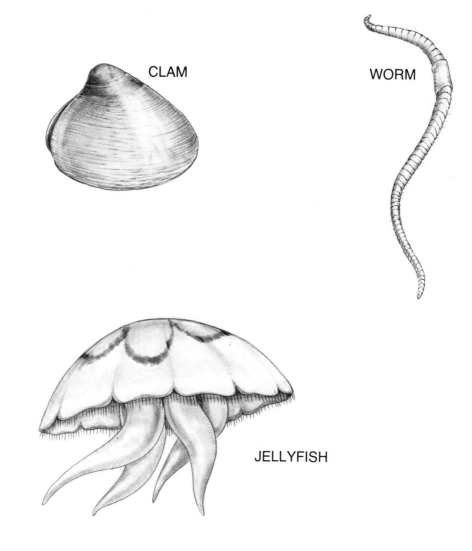

CLAM

WORM

JELLYFISH

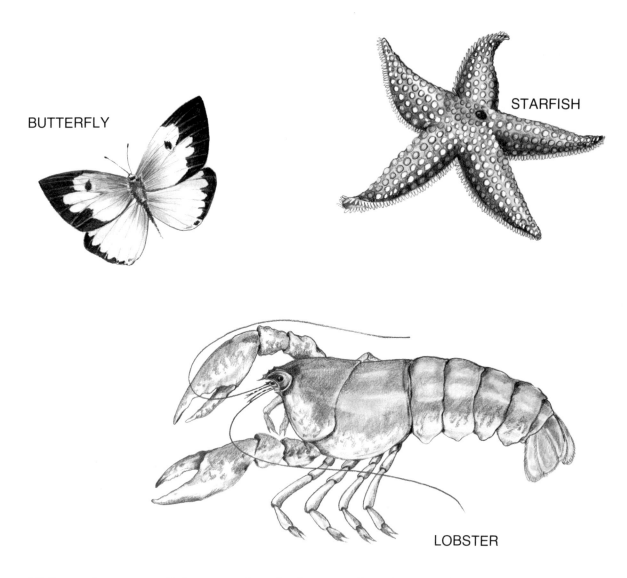

BUTTERFLY

STARFISH

LOBSTER

Although some of these animals have a hard outside covering, none of them have backbones.

They are called *in*vertebrates.

Now look at these animals.
They all have backbones.
They are all vertebrates.

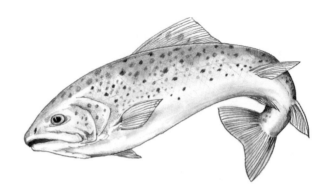

FISH

AMPHIBIANS   (am-FIB-ee-ans)

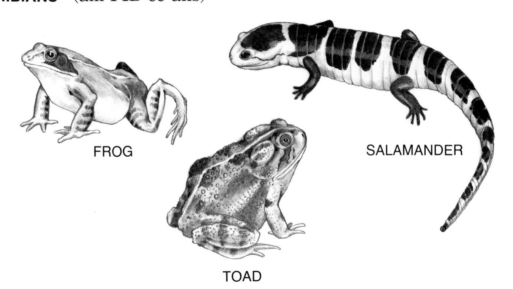

FROG

TOAD

SALAMANDER

REPTILES

SNAKE

TURTLE

LIZARD

BIRDS

MAMMALS

FISH

What makes a fish a fish?

A fish has a backbone.

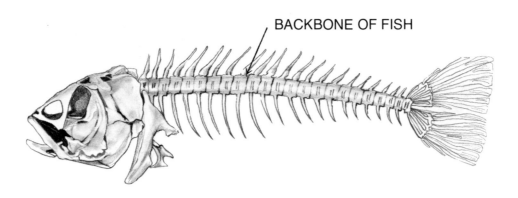

BACKBONE OF FISH

A fish breathes through gills and lives in water.

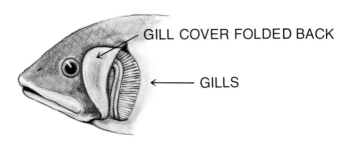

GILL COVER FOLDED BACK

GILLS

A fish has scales.

SCALES

The blood of a fish is always the same temperature
as the water it lives in.

TEMPERATURE OF WATER = 60°F

TEMPERATURE OF FISH = 60°F

And a fish has something no other animal has.
It has fins.

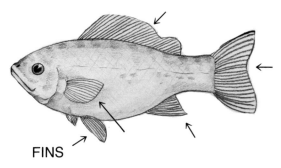

FINS

There are two big groups of fish.
Sharks and rays are in one group.
They have no real bones.
Their skeletons are made of cartilage (KAR-ti-lej),
which is softer than bone.

RAY

SHARK

It is easy to tell a shark from a ray.

The other group of fish has bones.
Most fish belong in this group.
You can tell these fish apart by looking
at the shape and the fins.

Which fish looks like a blimp?
Which fish has top fins that look like a comb?
Which fish looks like a snake?
Which fish has a tail fin like a V?

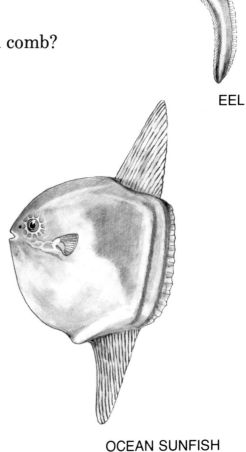

EEL

MACKEREL

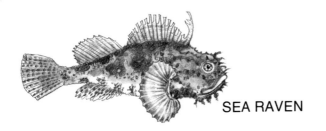

SEA RAVEN

OCEAN SUNFISH

AMPHIBIANS (am-FIB-ee-ans)

Frogs, toads, and salamanders are amphibians.
Amphibians have backbones.

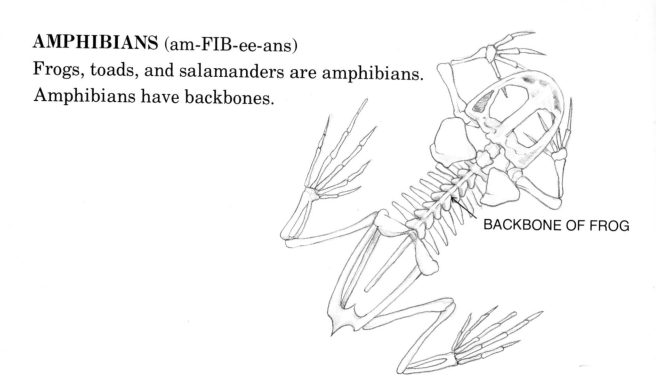

BACKBONE OF FROG

They lay their eggs in water
and spend the early part of their lives there.

A young amphibian is called a *tadpole*.
At first it has gills, but by the time it leaves the water,
it has lungs and can breathe the air on land.

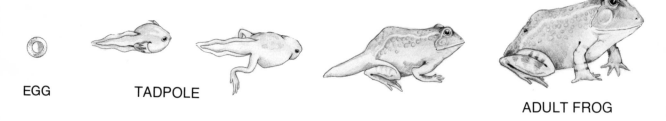

EGG   TADPOLE

ADULT FROG

16

Salamanders are amphibians with tails.

Frogs and toads are amphibians without tails.

Do you know how to tell a frog from a toad?
Look at the pictures.

TOAD   **FROG**

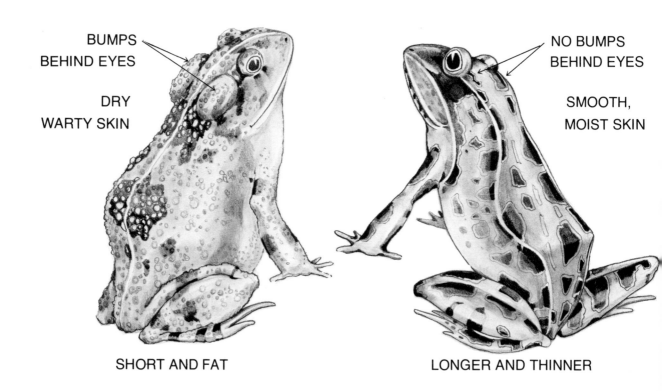

BUMPS
BEHIND EYES

DRY
WARTY SKIN

NO BUMPS
BEHIND EYES

SMOOTH,
MOIST SKIN

SHORT AND FAT   LONGER AND THINNER

Toads lay eggs in long strings.
Frogs lay eggs in clumps.

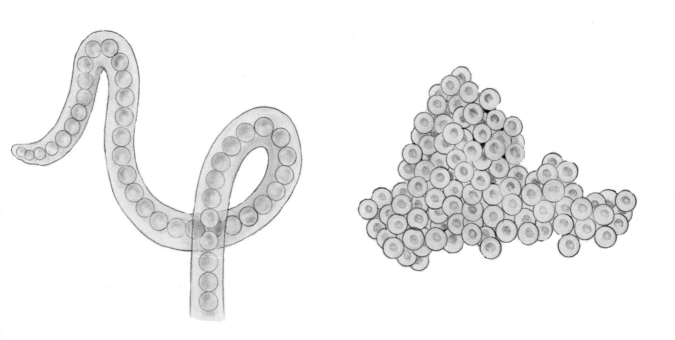

REPTILES

Snakes, lizards, turtles, and alligators are reptiles.
Reptiles have backbones.

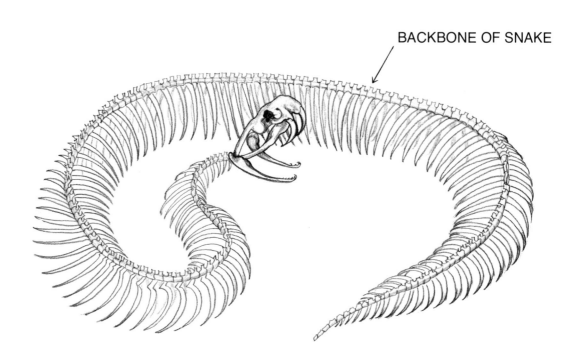

BACKBONE OF SNAKE

Like the fish, reptiles have scaly skins,
but these scales are tougher and harder.

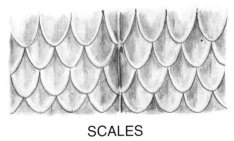

SCALES

Also reptiles do not have fins or gills.

The blood of reptiles is always the
same temperature as the air around it.

TEMPERATURE OF AIR = 80°F

TEMPERATURE OF REPTILE = 80°F

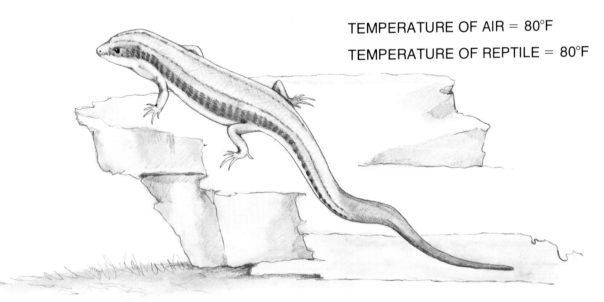

It is easy to tell reptiles apart.
Snakes have no legs.

Lizards look like snakes with legs.

Lizards have eyelids and ear openings.
Snakes do not.
Here are the heads of a snake and a lizard.
Which is which?

 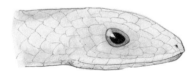

Alligators look like giant lizards.

Turtles are the only reptiles with shells.

BIRDS

What makes a bird a bird?

A bird has a backbone.

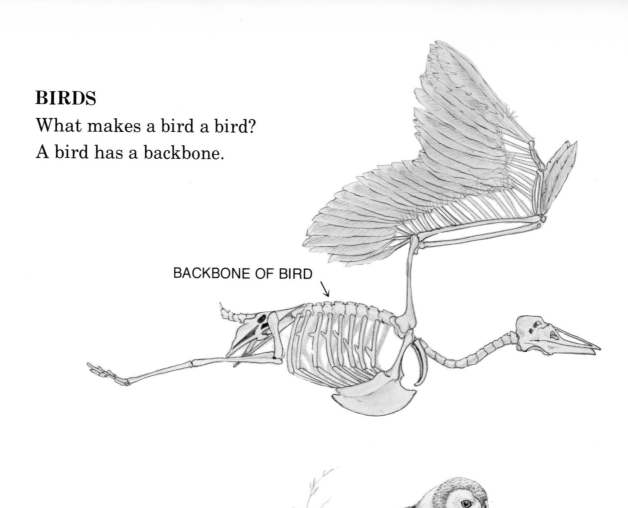

BACKBONE OF BIRD

A bird is warm-blooded.
Its blood stays warm even though
the temperature around it changes.

TEMPERATURE OF AIR = 40°F

TEMPERATURE OF BIRD = 102°

A bird usually flies.

And a bird has something no other animal has.
It has feathers.

SINGLE FEATHER

Birds can be told apart by their feet.

Birds that perch have three toes in front
and one long toe behind.
Find the perching toes.

Birds that walk have three long toes in front
and one short toe behind.
Find the walking toes.

Birds that swim have webbed feet.
Find the swimming toes.

Birds that climb have two toes in front
and two toes behind.
Find the climbing toes.

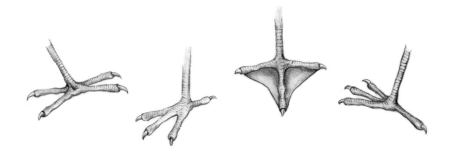

Birds are also told apart by their bills.

Birds with short, pointed bills usually eat insects.
Find the insect-eating bill.

Birds with short, thick, cone-shaped bills
usually crack seeds.
Find the seed-cracking bill.

Birds with hooked bills usually tear the flesh of small animals.
Find the flesh-tearing bill.

Birds with long, pointed bills usually catch fish.
Find the fish-eating bill.

MAMMALS

Animals with hair or fur are called mammals.

Mammals have backbones.

They are warm-blooded animals.

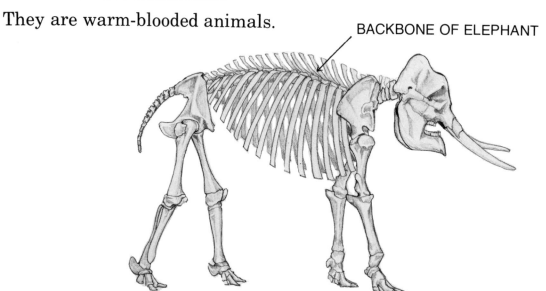

BACKBONE OF ELEPHANT

They also feed their babies milk from special parts
of their bodies called *mammary glands*.

Mammals are put in the same group
if they have the same kind of teeth.

Mammals that have sharp eyeteeth tear flesh.
Which are the flesh-tearing teeth?

Mammals that have two large front teeth on
top and bottom gnaw wood, nuts, and seeds.
Which are the gnawing teeth?

BEAVER

LION

Mammals are also told apart by their feet.

Some have three toes.

RHINOCEROS

Some have two toes.

PIG

Some have one toe.

HORSE

Some have no feet
but have flippers instead.

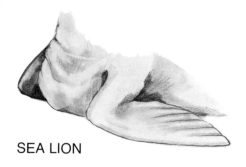

SEA LION

Some mammals have special parts that
no other mammal has.

An elephant has a trunk.

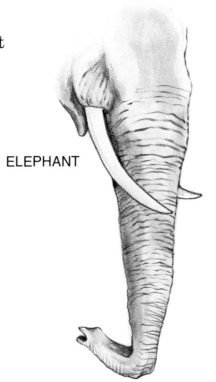

ELEPHANT

A bat has wings.

BAT

Mammals with large brains and hands that can grasp things
are in a special group.

MONKEY

31

HOW TO TELL THE VERTEBRATES APART:

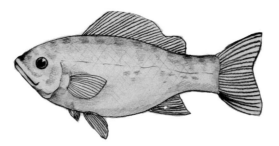

Fish have fins.

Amphibians lay their eggs in water
and spend the early part of their lives there.

Reptiles have scaly skins
but no gills or fins.

Birds have feathers.

Mammals have hair and feed their babies milk.

HIRAM HALLE MEM. (ROUND RIDGE)
J 596 S   30163602
Selsam, Millicent E.

026 022

J 596 S   40709
SELSAM, MILLICENT E
A FIRST LOOK AT ANIMALS
WITH BACKBONES

Hiram Halle Memorial Library